Seeds

by Jeffery L. Williams

HAMERAY
PUBLISHING GROUP

Published in the United States of America
by the Hameray Publishing Group, Inc.

Copyright © 2016 Hameray Publishing Group, Inc.

Publisher: Raymond Yuen
Editor: Tara Rodriquez
Cover Designer: Anita Adams
Book Designer: Stephani Rosenstein

Photo Credits: Page i – Xpixel; Page 2 – Marilyn Barbone;
Page 3 – Valentina Razumova; Page 4 – Xpixel; Page 5 – Annaev;
Page 6 – Aggie 11; Page 7 – Alena Root; Pages 8–9 – Blackzheep;
Page 10 – Successo Images; Page 11 – X4wiz; Page 12 – Africa
Studio; Page 13 – Zigroup-Creations; Page 14 – Julie Vader;
Pages 15–16 – Olga Popova

All rights reserved. No part of this publication may be reproduced or
transmitted in any form or by any means without permission in writing
from the publisher. Reproduction of any part of this book, through
photocopy, recording, or any electronic or mechanical retrieval system
without the written permission of the publisher, is an infringement of the
copyright law.

ISBN 978-1-62817-574-5

Printed in Singapore

2 3 4 5 6 7 8 IPS 23 22 21 20 19 18 17

Table of Contents

How plants grow from seeds 3

Kinds of seeds 10

Glossary 17

Index 18

Seeds are amazing.

How Plants Grow from Seeds
Every seed has a baby plant inside it.

The baby plant is waiting for three things to happen.

It goes into the dirt.

Water or rain falls on it.

It gets sunshine.

Then the seed can grow.

It grows and grows!

Kinds of Seeds

Some seeds are big. The seed of a coconut tree is a coconut.

It is as big as your head!

Some seeds are small. The seeds of a mustard plant are small.

They are about as big as
the period at the end of this
sentence.

Some seeds are **poisonous**. The seed of a buckeye tree is not good to eat. It would make you very sick.

Coconut seed

Pumpkin seeds

Sunflower seeds

Many seeds are not poisonous. We like to eat sunflower seeds, pumpkin seeds, and even coconut seeds.

Big or small, poisonous or not, seeds are amazing!

Glossary

poisonous: it will make you sick if you eat it

Index

buckeye, 14
coconut, 10–11, 15
dirt, 5
mustard seed, 12–13
pumpkin seed, 15
rain, 6
sunflower seed, 15
sunshine, 7
water, 6